Praise for *Another Land of My Body*

Why should a poet tell us what we already know? Rodney Terich Leonard's
poems frequently address the hidden, the overlooked, and the neglected. They
range from down South to men on the down-low, casting their inimitable
light on desire and family, on abandon and abandonment. Like the writers of
an earlier Harlem Renaissance, Leonard's poetry celebrates urban life while
maintaining a nourishing root in Black Southern communities and vernaculars.
And like those earlier writers, his poems upset the perceptions of a broken
and vicious nation: "Your language griot *cum laude.*" Always restless in place,
Leonard's gorgeous poetic portmanteau of postwar Black culture and history is
made to travel widely.
　—Alan Gilbert

Curtis Mayfield. Luther Vandross. Little Richard. Cousin Twyla. Uncle Douglas.
In his exciting sophomore collection, as though flipping through the thick,
laminated pages of old photo albums, Rodney Terich Leonard examines secrecy,
illness, loss, as well as the material conditions of Black people and their lived
experiences. Formally inventive, incantatory, and deeply musical, Leonard's
poems sing of the fullness of cultural experience, which include the violence we
are capable of inflicting upon one another and the violence inflicted upon Black
communities by structural racism and the state. Witting and lively, these lyrics
mourn, they celebrate, they charge us with the difficult task of remembering, of
saying the names of our beloved.
—Nathan McClain

Another Land of My Body

Also by Rodney Terich Leonard

Sweetgum & Lightning

Another Land of My Body

Rodney Terich Leonard

Four Way Books
Tribeca

Library of Congress Cataloging-in-Publication Data

Names: Leonard, Rodney Terich, author.
Title: Another land of my body / Rodney Terich Leonard.
Other titles: Another land of my body (Compilation)
Description: [New York] : [Four Way Books], 2024. |
Identifiers: LCCN 2023031708 (print) | LCCN 2023031709 (ebook) | ISBN
9781954245945 (trade paperback) | ISBN 9781954245952 (ebook)
Subjects: LCGFT: Poetry.
Classification: LCC PS3612.E5744 A85 2024 (print) | LCC PS3612.E5744
(ebook) | DDC 811/.6--dc23/eng/20230824
LC record available at https://lccn.loc.gov/2023031708
LC ebook record available at https://lccn.loc.gov/2023031709

This book is manufactured in the United States of America and printed on
acid-free paper.

Four Way Books is a not-for-profit literary press. We are grateful for the assistance
we receive from individual donors, public arts agencies, and private foundations
including the NEA, and the New York State Council on the Arts, a state agency.

We are a proud member of the Community of Literary Magazines and Presses.

Contents

Uppity & Spacious

What Unravels Here Has Sprouts

Winter Was Houndstooth

Another Land of My Body

Uppity & Spacious

Airman's Diary:
The Angel I Encountered on the Train Platform

Sunday, October 13, 1991
RAF Woodbridge
Suffolk, East Anglia, England

Sometimes it's a ribbon in the sand

Captivated by your ankle;

it Bojangles next to your chair.

Or the frequency of neon technologics:

11:11 on the clock.

11/11 on the cell.   11-11 in argon on the hull of a ship.

Haint is a wind word.   She was there and not there.

Comparatively there,

Based on my prior brushes with abandonment.

Prone to brittle & into conjure,

I'm convinced of an Eye that chiefs over me.

Concerning Cousin Twyla

Her front door has no screen.

She sells her moon to men.

When jittery in mittens

Whom of Harriet Tubman's ilk,

Such a glory over everything

Assured her, mint of breath:

I am your parakeet.

Lift   your   head

Lofty among the bricks

Of the Springhill Projects.

Her pain is checkered.

Her pain is not strange.

Which of her gossiping aunts

Sought permission to unravel?

Raised a village mountainous

As Septima Poinsette Clark?

Each braid furthers us.

Look over here—

Toward a second-hand heart.

Breeze on my back

I'm unfit to sling the hammer.

Snippets As Per Two Scorpio Poets: (a)

Montrachet & Filet de Boeuf, Béarnaise?

Cigarettes tucked in socks can be sexy.

*

All the backed-up trucks & vacant limos.

I lived high enough past May to feel grown.

*

Yellow-striped, back-of-the-truck nectarines.

Why is everything rural with you?

*

The Colonel sang *when hope was high and life…*

Aretha had a four-day funeral.

*

Cold heels claimed cold heels tagged cold heels claimed cold.

Alexa: Luther "Dance with My Father."

*

Would you say our rancor is beige Gucci?

Gucci: yes, rad & all that but not beige.

*

If or not to twerk it 'til you make it?

Mixed tapes & carrying-on comes to mind.

Snippets As Per Two Scorpio Poets: (A)

Sherry or Nova Scotia halibut?
I've reckoned with cigarettes tucked in socks.

*

Tom Ford Extreme or Fucking Fabulous?
Neither neither neither neither neither!

*

Yellow-meat off-the-truck watermelons?
Rather red my lips with looted MAC stuff.

*

Sister Tuck sang *over troubled water...*
Obsequies for Miss Breonna Taylor.

*

Heels cold cold-heeled history heels claimed cold:
Ahmaud Arbery—George Floyd—Rayshard Brooks.

*

If or not to cough turning death's corner?
Don't ask me shit about when I might cough.

After Alpharetta, Salvador, Bahia

—let's give it up for port lovers

Jingle swell jingle hell jingle all of May.
Sound is a sorority.
The lone bangle doesn't jiggle.

Little Richard & Prince wore pink-a-bye pumps.
Neither lassoed my torso like Phoebe Snow.
Do you know Phoebe Snow?

I met Phoebe, in black & white,
Trilling a Sears jingle.
After the George Floyd rally it rained in Alpharetta.
After the rally we heard "Every Night":

I lean on a lamp post,
I'm wasting my time.

In this crumpled impossibility of Georgia—
No stair in the townhouse to claim
Sorrow grows & grows
Lonely like a wooden bowl
Still eating meat with bad teeth
Phoebe Snow is eighty, burgundy, top-pressed sheets.

Look at him brush his pretty waves with a black brush.
I used to pick at stank used to be a mender this is so booty.

Abracadabra!

And where do I jet to when I need love?
To Salvador, Bahia—
To samba in Barra
With that goateed bassist.

Under the Ambiance of Shirley Horn's "Meaning of the Blues"

Blue was just a ribbon for first prize 'till...
— Julie London

When a batch of gimlets:

Tito's
Simple syrup & fresh-squeezed lime

Steamed chicken gyoza
Crispy orange chicken

&

Bitter broccoli rabe
Mimic the last torso I clutched

It's time for some.
           Far from shame—

Better than sleeping with clients.

Bless the threshold by crossing it;

I will pay.

Jintz: A Warrior Woman: The Way a Story About Someone Else Just Nails It

for worldwide women warriors
for them warriors

i.

Mr. Elijah and Mrs. Earline Jones
Were the threads and gold of marriage.
The sun that Sunday as much theirs
As Saturday's had been.
A rock meant indeed to Mrs. Earline.
Squabble dragged from porch-poured
Coffee to Peace and Goodwill Baptist.
Mr. Elijah—not soothed by chancel
Couldn't snuff the argument.
He nagged & his nags grew hair.
Simmering from the jump,
Mrs. Earline—boiled to a lisp—squealed:
Hell if I wouldn't.   Lijah—
If I had a wock I'd a knock ya out.
Hollers seesawed the pews.

ii.

I am shook by the names of these Igneous rocks:
Adakite.   Basanite.   Blairmorite.
Diorite.   Gabbro.   Kimberlite.   Lherzolite.

You're a rock—
Sachet of neem.
A tangible leaning post.
Niche to weigh intuition.
Grip for the gable.
Your language griot *cum laude*.

Alfred Charles Sharpton, Jr.

        Dreamt which hole
Best oils the skeleton key.

The hot of his name
Chaps & blisters Mitch McConnell's lips.

        Reverend Al—

Brooklyn's Brownsville Gospeler.
Gent of slick-brutality sermons.

Wade into his mosaic eyes.
They're off-red & over-rallied.

        Or glimpse Ruleville—

The gold of Sister Fannie Lou Hamer's
Tooth frowning at ya.

Remember the fluffy perm & FUBU sweats?
He was James Brown's road manager.

Summer hips every Black man to chrysanthemums.

Uppity & Spacious

Besides a wasp in the shutters
Otherwise unalarmed as glycerin
I awake to ocean & dunes
To uppity cerulean
San José Cabo sky.

I wish my grandmother owned Zadún, a Ritz-Carlton Reserve.
I underline the thought.
I swear I care.
Where is my pied-à-terre?
What's a wall without a Kerry James Marshall?

Overnight broiled to randy
9am wands me expressed.
I glide into that kingdom of tub facing north.
I am ready for me this Fourth of July.
I soak & play in lavender & orange peels.

I loofah & keep it keen.
Today is dedicated to Curtis Mayfield
For penning *Eddie You Should Know Better*.
Spacious sky: I summered with a man named Obie.

On Missing Miss Aretha Franklin

since August 16, 2018

Rasp scat or mid-phrase moan,
Aretha could lock her lids
& unfasten everybody's sentiment.

Amazing Grace oiled her throttle
For Ebenezer Baptist & primetime.
Of cape—of gown—or strapless

Of Big Band & Steinway by ear.
Galloping octaves—
She sang *Skylark*.

What Unravels Here Has Sprouts

And We Try to Find Gestures for Our Humanity When We're Young

She's behaving midnight again.
Her bedroom blinds shut.
The installation of quilted drapes.
Scribbling *J.T.* repeatedly on notepads.
This is when I grease her scalp.
What a harvest—
Mounds of envelopes on the nightstand.
Before opioids were news.
This is her green house—

Rot plowed from the root,
what unravels here has sprouts.
Galatians verbatim on her tongue;
her children—Amen, Amen—
are starched in the eyes of God.
She wears her own hair & Fashion Fair.
Stutter ignores her penchant
For fried whiting & hushpuppies.
No one I know calls her baby.

But this isn't a portrait
of the patient slow-dancing,
ambulance parked in the driveway.
Here is a woman as monument;

the flash for this sitting was gratuitous.
Her legacy is how not to ask for much:
"Give a child what you can and fertilize it."
My mother's allure wasn't from a magazine;
Jet came later.

House of Five:
Five Folks Living Up in There with One Fan

After oxtails, white rice
Cabbage, mac & cheese
Stuffing & two cold Cokes

Belly bulge belly particular
The narcissist yells

I need the fan on high

Turn the *fan* on high

Turn the fan on high

Tilt it my way

I am displeased

Poverty

They refuse to call it violence.

Summer carnivals huddle to tempt the poor.

Pay the children with sugar & crumbs.

Snatch the penny candy. Lick your mama's cake bowl.

My sister "lost" eight boxes of Girl Scout Thin Mints.

I got a jug of Jolly Ranchers for Christmas.

'Tis the hour you're born or unborn slick.

With or without muscularity for lack.

There is no bread.

Today's canned tuna fish is without bread.

The field trip costs three dollars.

Do you have three dollars?

The fare can't be split with a cousin.

You know what they say about each tub's bottom.

Every child wonders why, but why?

Maw rhymes with claw—

My name rhymes with X

And the xylophone I play.

I couldn't be clawed by poverty.

My arms had to be themselves.

Would you want a lamp lit without its globe?

My Friend, Ty, Cuts My Former Boss's Hair at Frank E. Campbell—The Funeral Chapel

Greeted with bows & salutations.
Cash counted yesterday,
I ask for a pre-peek of the meadow.
For a mental splash of the salon
To which we, the barber & I, are headed.

We step off the gold-gated elevator
And exchange Black-looks 1:
See herds of settees & wingback chairs.
Sun cousins its way around the room.

And then we Black-looks 2:
See a stocked bar cart.
Bucketed Brut.
We could fart.

I wonder if anyone's ever puckered
Or hollered out
Or needed ammonia
Or a handkerchief in here?

Three evenings ago
Twelve floor-to-ceiling windows dim the East River.
Flanked by nurses & cellists

The long-legged Mr. was sundowning.
Today he is semi-ready;
Cream-rose nostrils & hands, buffed nails,
Starched, white, crewneck tee.
Upon a slab draped with attentive black pleats.
In-process, laid out.
Hear Bach.

Between snips
Ty muses:
"This set-up is dope as shit.
Was G a Mason?
I have to remember this Black man's name."

On Four Seasons Hotel Stationery:
New York Downtown

Please dust everything above & below the TV.

Everything wood—

Banquette, Beds, Blinds.

It's Thursday, deep-clean everywhere.

Both Living Rooms. The Bathrooms.

The Kitchen & Bedrooms.

The Floors & Crevices. Water the Piano

& do the Laundry:

Clothes, Sheets, Towels.

Noreen—

I shouldn't have to tell you

That Vlad's & Primo's water bowls smell rearish,

Like mouth.

Sniff them & wash thoroughly with vinegar!

This is important:

Please mind Richard's wig stands; last week one was toppled.

XOXO—You're always needed

Little Swan & *The Real Housewives of Atlanta*

Haven't you needlessly wadded

Handfuls of each other's hair & wigs & weaves?

A little girl named Swan

Eyes her father acrobat her mother's

Hair taking her to clogged wells

Where episodes go to grimace

& around midnight, it's lights out, not television.

Swan is six & mimics NeNe Leakes.

Swan—evening-eats Cheerios.

Whimpers for fake fluorescent nails.

Housewives—

Pain—rests not upon pillows—is a sea.

Your real & rehearsed tantrums.

Relatable reality.

Bay County police on speed dial,

Her mother finally flipped the channel.

Charlie Rose: The rise and plummet of a man who preached 'character' and 'integrity'

—*The Washington Post*, Nov. 21, 2017

Charlie,

A bough for issues for terrain.

With whom I scurried past Dixie
Past Tuscaloosa past prejudice.

With whom I jounced nightly
For bling & insight—

In 1993,
After Maya Angelou's inaugural

"On the Pulse of Morning,"
Swell as Le Creuset

Twin of giggle at the table
With those lowball glasses

Sipping seltzer or something
He egged & she wisped

"Wouldn't
Take Nothing for My Journey Now."

A catcher's mitt.
Eight women.
Eight-plus accusations.
Caught sniffing your itch.

Man-Low

a Black idiom with universal, all-o'-y'all, application

Impacted by posture & circumstance

While wholly operating from the ego.

Man-low in a sentence:

Unable & unwilling to bury his mother,
he is feeling & behaving really man-low.

After Years of Watching Them Be Them, I've Still Got This Fire

My side of the seesaw on the ground
I loved a white man beyond the silver's worth.
White cat swigging Glenlivet in my crib
The subject of President Obama got his goat.
He split without his hat & we hollered.
Another white man chortled
That he's white when it comes to money.

After I bathed him
The white man tried to shoo & stiff me—
Buck-eyed from Tuscaloosa
I sounded my switchblade on 86th & Park
In the laryngologist's powder room.
Me & my wild locs headed to Paris:
Onto the 777 walked another airline's captain
For whom my crew ID was null.
Me & my wild locs (in Paris we) oyster at Au Rocher de Cancale.

Where to flush this?
That campus of Northeastern Ivy w/o a Drum & Bugle Corps
I sicced my government shrink
On two fine brains of that department.
Maître d, bartenders, big Manager's
All male & white—

No matter the gratuity no redemption at Majorelle;

A Last Word is $24.00. $62 grilled salmon à la carte.

And to the faux hawk privileged editor:

Suds from the wash collapse in the rinse.

Verified & disarmed—

I still see my grandfather crawling down the Edyburns hill.

Nary a Thimble for Young Sadness

for Nigel Shelby, 2004-2019

(Huntsville. Gay & out & bullied.
"Suffered from depression." Rested in a rainbow-covered casket.)

Born under the same moon, counties & storms apart
This scar above my ribs, the geography of people
 yanking me for being me.

Nary a thimble for young sadness.
I reaped a few acres about Alabama.
About phobic attraction to sizzle
& sameness & welts.

Wide fields raise itching ivy.
I never met Governor George Wallace.

Pardon Auburn's genial Buicks & clowns.
Born in November of '70,
Clowns didn't spook my generation.
But, place can blister.

Nigel—

I am sorry that April hid its prance.
18th of April. You were an Aries. Rams usually scrape.
Were there premonitions?
Pasture dreams of three-leaf clovers?

Did you suddenly have a taste for Rotel dip or collards?
You were fifteen & knocking.
And too on-the-vine to plumb
That woe, when sipped & treated, is not lethal.

Your mother said you were sunshine.
Sunshine embarrasses some mothers.

I Was Trent & Shit for Trent Got Janky

Blood in sputum.
Nodular underneath the turtleneck.

Redacted medical records.
Patient is twenty-six & zapped.

The red ribbon blight
Maimed as hands
Sorrily stitched remembrance quilts.

Sepia-fooled
Groove-swept
Men tenderized me.

My only thorn with dying
Is parting with the beats.

After the Memorial Cremate Me
in Green & Black

Starch the asparagus cutaway collar.
Work my grandfather's large-knots blue-green tie.

                    Wrap my head Leontyne-like.
          Skirt me in Black linen from the waist down.

Onyx toe ring to max me out.
Empress of ingredient gowns,

Appoint Kyemah McEntyre to inspect me.
                Harpists for poets & cocktails.

Heaps of affected peonies.
              Black casket sealed.

Winter Was Houndstooth

Crooked Aura

Old-wig-like,

Our aura is askew.

The cadence of same ole triggers no flutter.

This boarding pass ridged on page twelve

Of a bargain, of the rinse—

"If He Hollers Let Him Go."

Used to be each other's crease.

Winter was houndstooth.

In a moister world,

The last of the stardust flurried.

My nails were freckled teal.

Harlem Artists Salon

When my duplex   & art salons were swollen   all-night-blue
                      Non-BYOB affairs   & I was simply

Donning my upbringing   Overpouring & puffing

Un-teaching myself that applause can be bought—

Your hands   cupped the peony stems & spruced the parlor
                  More Midwestern & bright.

& after the pukers
        & highbrows left
                Esther Phillips was chamomile.
                    The swallows lengthened us—

Eggs, cayenne grits
& Conecuh sausage
On bamboo half-plates.
Then came the knee & winded stuff.

Whenever I'm in Los Feliz
Attached & pinned

To this new glare of mine
That you mattered matters.

But Beautiful

Beauty brings copies of itself into being.
—Elaine Scarry, *On Beauty and Being Just*

Apple orchard limb-jubilant tree
Fuji aplomb for every belly.
A hungry man's happy-red moan
Quicker you pluck 'em quicker they gone.
Grandma's been fly for years
Kodak'ed once between her tears.
Teeth brushed of corn & snuff
Jet-black beehive mauve powder puff—
In a nectarine high-draped skirt.

Pool-hall juke Big Maybelle
Stereo-stewed hog maws to quell.
The gent of lower crooked tooth
Bedford-Stuyvesant's claim to hoof.
Without a mate is neo-angular
The whiff of weed leaps rectangular.
I'm about to flip not quite qualm
Scant time for frangipani or psalm—
Beauty bucked me for renting love.

Precious, Precious, Don't Be Fooled

Rethink the flat ass.
Peek-a-boo—

        Between the mounds
Dig the deluxe interior.

Another Land of My Body

An abrupt ravine.

I learned another land of my body.

Packaged trauma—

Eleven orchids refusing mist.

Maimed to the bone.

Texture of asphalt shingles;

He rocked a red cap backwards.

My pinkie strolled across corduroy.

Grown shame is shame groomed.

Here I can't say what I sometimes crave.

Hunger is one of my songs.

Once Between Sets at Bemelmans Bar

The marble floors in the Carlyle loo:

Have they been waxed since March?

Unmounted Crabtree & Evelyn

& cotton hand towels.

Oh to be charged & trusted like this!

The night the pink pocket square meant skank:

Two untamed beards in the far-left stall.

Warm-warm post-martini mouth;

                                 Artful froth.

Lint silvered the air vents.

Interval air fresheners bleeped wild,

goading us on, spit-rich, as if to say,

"Get it get it."

Nice, France: Les Bains-Douches

Go 'head
Abraham
Hava nagila hava—
Girth of Tel Aviv.

I breathe breathe
Breathe breathe
Diaphragmatically—
Relaxed sac of Czech.

Sauna steam triphop,
Quinn—
Dandy as Fahrenheit.
Bristol's don't-hurry.

Monaco pec shop—
Has he ever eaten grease?
Ridgeless & smooth
& smooth betwixt.

My guess is Fez.
Towel-tucked
Pique intrigue—
Three is company.

Rotterdam—
Ride in my Mercedes boy
Leanly
Like it is.

PAUSE don't make no sense.
Mic check—
Cape Town derrière;
Shiloh I-want-in.

Sheraton's Pleated Roman Shades Rolled All-the-Way Up

They-to-They.
Chest-to-Chest.
Santiago cuddling us.

Poem for Lifetime Eaters of Pig, Pintos & Cornbread

for Miss Maxine Royal

Forever floral on the dance floor
Past the hustle & rocking chair
Past Peaches & Herb & the Smurf
Beyond *Soul Train* routines
Down yonder by the funky chicken

Maxine's jiggle bloomed on skates.
Maxine's jiggle blew the speakers.

Envy at the Blue Moon Drive—
                 She's peerless
In a purple, wonder-wonderful catsuit.
Hips dissed by pig, pintos & cornbread
Hips that'll never dominate a mattress
Such hip-envy at the Blue Moon Drive;
Oh to have hips under-shaped by God.

                Miss Maxine's jiggle
Asked men in the club

Can you handle this announcement?
Can you pick the locks on these planets?

Spirit of Phlegm

On the Seventh Night: a Brew, a Spell

The moon is neither jester nor distended.

I come to the water   unhyphenated   irreverent
          Ready for combat
                    The heirs renege
Have ruffled my feathers   There were *two* contracts

But the verbal part died when the Mr. died. Hold on died when the
Mr. died. Hold on died when the Mr. died. Hold on died when the
Mr. died. Hold on died when the Mr. died. Hold on died when the
Mr. died. Hold on died when the Mr. died. Hold on—

                    I want my money!

I can't point to the water or mouth what water is or is not.
I was handed a big bronze bell.
My grandfather handed me this spell.

          *

Break & boil leaves & yellow root in cast iron
      Add initials of the damned on white paper to unkink kinks
Channel the ride-or-die departed:

Aunt Catherine   big & Black chews mackerel
Nods eastward   weeps & claps 1-1-1-1
Initials & kinks a-boiling:
M   D   A L S M
        L EM DAS AALDM   S   L

*

Ah! Annie Alexander!
Her gravy-smothered garlic steak & tiered red velvet cake.
Dear cousin
Buried in brown:
Foundation   wig   brooch   dress

Ludicrous   snuff-layered lashes
Long-loose lavender dress.

*

Sister Elezie
Hilltop abbess
Mothball bracelet
Outhorns the foghorn
Spirit of phlegm

Phlegms:

Unjar the green worms
Don't be careful
Boil the leaves
Stir the initials & area codes again

M   D   A L   S   M
**   L E   410**

202   212   323 221 014   220

Cough! Cough! Cough!
Repeat after me
In the absence of the wooden wife & daughter
In the presence of the rich & adopted daughter
You fluffed the tycoon's pillow
Wiped catarrh from the tall man's bib
Stir towards your money
Then sip then use your tongue & you sip

*

Ringing the big bronze bell
Ringing the big bronze bell

Ringing the big bronze bell
4—.
Ringing the big bronze bell
Ringing the big bronze bell
Ringing the big bronze bell
7—.
Ringing the big bronze bell

I sip   & sip &   sip the
                    Yellow Roux.

On the Eve of the 2020 Presidential Election:
On the Eve of Defeat

Donald J. Trump
Shook like a Rottweiler
Shitting knife-shaped
Persimmon seeds. *

*The shape of the kernels predicts winter weather.

Low Cs

In this season of clots
Craniectomy & compression
Jeaning the curve to 50
Seems to nudge to stomach
No more bologna
No more flitch
No more Red Hots & oil sausage
No more head-flesh cheese
Canned meatballs & red soda.
Blood-blocking buddies, farewell.
Pickles, onions, mayo, mustard
A big juicy burger was rapture.
A shift before the hemorrhagic stroke,
McDonalds.
What's next isn't boojee:
Diapered for 19 days.
Skull bone refrigerated.
Weaned from Propofol,
Non-crying Caleb cried near the end.

Upon PTSD: Notes after psychotherapy, a maintenance session

He heard the Army would straighten him out.
He dreamed a she & two unborn babies
Would straighten him out.
No hiding place.

There's a new mole on my face.
Air in my spirit
Near the ledge I'm carefree.
I'm reading *The Book of Symbols*.
Being handed a note that widens the eyes.
We don our parents; better not call them liars.

Alzheimer's Disease

Taking with it names, dates, manners
Tunes, flirtation & folded certificates

> The rink of memory skating swell
> Into a dancehall of repeats & swears

To Tremble with Questions

Text From a U-Shaped Valley

Doll face,
Meet Ruby, my youngest sister & highest card.
I brought her up-to-date about my condition.
With our first-cousin's wake next Monday,
Mom's ammonia cloth is folded in her purse.
Let's not mention vinegar just yet.
If my pallor worsens—blare the horn.
Though I am not COVID-confirmed,
The Brooklyn VA forbids visitors.
NYC is a blooming cemetery; stay put.
C is my power-of-attorney
Health-care proxy & Executor-of-Estate.
I'm a brim in a brook about pity.
I have flexed & amplified "in the along" of life.
Please advocate for my nimble crossover. DNR.
Don't prolong the chafe: kibosh & bounce.
This won't be news for C:
There is guidance in PDF & a green folder:
Entrust Frank E. Campbell—The Funeral Chapel.
Direct cremation. No viewing! It whelms
That I postponed prefacing my life to family.
I am sorry for this cement.
And yet of grace on this pneumatic bed
Ogun asks for no snails or palm oil—

Love is sippable. This valley, U-shaped.
Get to know each other.
I need brawn & full-named prayers.

I've Known Salt: This to Gray

This could be the end of sleeved Saturdays.
Saturday last—
Self-cornered in vintage Halston
At Red Rooster Harlem:
"Sidecar, cutes, no rim."
It's Stephen Sondheim's 90th.
Isn't it queer? Losing my timing this late…
Feel me feeling a lyric.
Nonstop from kindred to prophetic,
Feel me rewind a lyric
Losing my timing this late
In Brooklyn at the VA hospital.

50/50: Hypoxic Respiratory Failure.
Beloved—
Pay your nickel.
Away from waiting rooms
Fret elsewhere.
Sweat Almighty Sweat.
I hear this thing eats brain.
Got a Black scarf to wrap my head.
Gray streaks. Gray circles. Elk gray.
Everything I see does something gray.
Ends in gray. Gray swallows. Gray gas.

I do not remove my turban.

Wattage in my armpits.
I've known salt.
If only I could jot.
Brook nervous,
I can't un-itch my armpits.
Bashful light in here.
I blare the call bell from noon to 3.
I smell dried rind & skunk.
I get back on that bell.
These bitches won't answer.
Gray biceps.
Alone in this building palpitate to gray.

*

The ninety-sixth hour of shivers.
Next to me are two classy
Black Andalusian horses.
Eighth drenching onward.
Un-socked soles ablaze
Up & down hallucination's pole
I forgot I had an Iphone.

Carlos's prod is pukka:
What's with the visiting horses?
Don't upset the nurses.
I can't quite breathe.
I'm on therapeutic oxygen.

Air is lost inside me.
Carlos Zooms me to the toilet.
I crawl & shit everywhere.
Gratitude on my tongue.
Gratitude for wee, sacred breaths.
Mariachi in Mexico City; heads or tails?
Tails: This is not last January.
Carlos is stern:
Stay above the layer. Stay above it.
Roger that!
I become a bird & bust out of my cage.
I'm an ostrich.
My mien is gutbucket.

In backless gown & sneakers
Important tote on my shoulder
I am pale, thinner.
I am Zeus & full of shit again.

Zeus busts loose. Out of quarantine!
As if the ribs she chewed turned to bone,
The rotund desk nurse ran & squealed.
She busted loose down the corridor.
Zeus locates the elevator.
Zeus makes it to the ground level.
Zeus is masked & cold.
Zeus is confused & not confused.

Antipruritic my pits.
I am dying.
Glory is for old folks.
I am whisked & wheeled back upstairs.
I am scolded.
I don't give a damn.

Oh, I get loud.
I don't budge until I swallow a sedative.
In the hallway.
Amor in crisis.   Do I have COVID?
Death must court me.
I am a gentleman.

*

Morning had a restless night.
Per my pillows & sheets.
Per the night pill.
Per the bloodletting.
Mind my wishes.
I get up, get dressed,
Ring the nurse's station & hear:
This this crazy-ass dude that walked outta
His room late last night his ass all out.
We outta sheets.
Doctors make their rounds soon.
                              Click!

I guess he told me.
Labs six days late.

Pneumonia brewed, six days, at least.
Brewed & untreated.
Do I have COVID?

                    *

Late Noon: The Dr. Arrives & Speaks

"I love your turban.   I smell lemongrass.
Do you know you're dying?   Let me take care of you.
Do you know you're dying?   Why do you want to die?
I hear that last night was rough for you.   We are all afraid.
You're ill so please don't leave.   Who is Carlos?
If you leave here you will die tonight."

You Might Need Somebody
You might need somebody too.

*

How far away is the ambulette?

I discharge myself against medical advice.

Having served in America's wars
Commanded to be straight
Why would I expect the VA Hospital
The antlers of the nation
To merit my life & limbs
In limbo in peril?

74

*

Later that evening.
Another hospital.
Low ground east of the Mississippi.

(It's me again): I:
Hyperventilate.
Piss myself.
Pull out my IVs.
Blood made me.
Oxygen saturation: 62.
The last man I see is a Cypress.
Smells like cedar.
Once on the pipe: 4-3-2-

*

                    Ventilators
Renovate obligations.

Now I pack my tote for bat terrain:
Palo Santo
Bronze African bell

Pine Oil

Black Adinkra prayer shawl

Would rather be winded than morgued.

Lenox Hill Hospital: Uris 7612

Away from the window
Cooped nearest the loo
Roomed with Mr. Waxman:
Nurse! Nurse! I wanna die!
I, too, am hymning.
I'm giving this American Standard
The Best of the Trots.

In concert—
I scan my labs for oddity:
C-Reactive Protein: 2.26
D-Dimer Levels: 8332.
Inflammation & blood clots;
Medical-mask & hot face Emoji.
I croon on.

Azithromycin   Ensure
Hydroxychloroquine
Lasix   Lorazepam
Lovenox   Pepcid
Tylenol & Vegetable Broth
Have dubbed me
Egesta.

Intravenous Sashay:
Having Asked for Something to Ease My Anxiety

Rookie to morphine:

Maya Angelou

Pedals a green tricycle.

One Wall Away a Woman Dies of COVID-19

"Uncle Nestor Uncle Nestor Uncle Nestor Uncle
Nestor Uncle Nestor Uncle Nestor Uncle Nestor
Uncle Nestor Uncle Nestor Uncle Nestor Uncle
Nestor Uncle Nestor Uncle Nestor Uncle Nestor
Uncle Nestor Uncle Nestor Uncle Nestor Uncle
Nestor Uncle Nestor Uncle Nestor Uncle Nestor
Uncle Nestor Uncle Nestor Uncle Nestor Uncle
Nestor Uncle Nestor Uncle Nestor Uncle Nestor
Uncle Nestor Uncle Nestor Uncle Nestor Uncle
Nestor Uncle Nestor Uncle Nestor Uncle Nestor
Uncle Nestor Uncle Nestor Uncle Nestor Uncle
Nestor Uncle Nestor Uncle Nestor Uncle Nestor
Uncle Nestor Uncle Nestor Uncle Nestor Uncle
Nestor Uncle Nestor Uncle Nestor Uncle Nestor
Uncle Nestor Uncle Nestor Uncle Nestor Uncle
Nestor Uncle Nestor Uncle Nestor Uncle Nestor
Uncle Nestor Uncle Nestor Uncle Nestor Uncle
Nestor Uncle Nestor Uncle Nestor Uncle Nestor
Uncle Nestor Uncle Nestor Uncle Nestor Uncle
Nestor Uncle Nestor Uncle Nestor Uncle Nestor
Uncle Nestor Uncle Nestor Uncle Nestor Uncle
Nestor Uncle Nestor Uncle Nestor Uncle Nestor

Uncle Nestor Uncle Nestor Uncle Nestor Uncle
Nestor Uncle Nestor Uncle Nestor Uncle Nestor
Uncle Nestor Uncle Nestor Uncle Nestor Uncle
Nestor Uncle Nestor Uncle Nestor Uncle Nestor
Uncle Nestor Uncle Nestor Uncle Nestor Uncle
Nestor Uncle Nestor Uncle Nestor Uncle Nestor
Uncle Nestor Uncle Nestor Uncle Nestor Uncle
Nestor Uncle Nestor Uncle Nestor Uncle Nestor
Uncle Nestor Uncle Nestor Uncle Nestor Uncle
Nestor Uncle Nestor Uncle Nestor Uncle Nestor."

In the ward of perpetual gnash—
Semi-Delirium & Delirium.

What a final infection.
One wall away,
I hear her swerve the plateau.

Uncle Douglas: He Showed Out & Left

Gripped from the chair
Flashed in front of a .38
How do you flinch
Undid   This is bad news.
You eyeball him
Pee your dungarees
You're five.
He is a tornado
Foaming at the mouth
Never again
To be irked for butterscotch.

Auntee hugs me twice.
Her breathing
Bounces back to skillets.
Twelve children smell cornbread.
                    COVID-19—
Via a red megaphone:
Day 10 beeps URGENT.
You're into lungs & dyspnea.
Where are my calves?
I, of eyeball, was born a secret.
Stranger to these pines,

You won't un-timber me.

You can't just cut through Nixburg, Alabama.

Ms. Clematine & Ms. Bessie Will
of Rockford & Alexander City, Alabama

Quick sad corridor care without Kleenex & wipes.
They paid taxes in an American town with six ICU beds.

The Mighty Grip:

COVID pumped up on these sisters
  With their pre-Parkinson's
    & hypertension
      pileups
        & COPD
          at ages 75 & 86
& the heirloom chitlins
  & pound cake recipes
    & summer-white buckets of Budweiser
      To B.B. King went hush.

   *

Six days of drawn-out things.
A day dry-of-a-week.
Six ICU beds.
Clematine trucked to Flowers Hospital in Dothan.
Bessie Will refused Mobile.
Bessie Will went home & gasped.

Organ aura at the service.

Crooked forward march for the family.

We wired twin, hot-pink sprays.

To Tremble with Questions

My moan is the sound of faith
Upwards of gut.

No nurse or doctor explains the substitute
For a final spoon of honey on the tongue.

This Means I Won't Sip Here Again

for Dr. Obie Nichols

Stainless fridge ten-months shut.

                        Ten months stale   Lickety-split,

My friend.

Salmon still smells of basil.

Snifter moist with chill   Mashy eggplant water

                              A third of a pecan pie

          Two bites

Of turkey & Swiss.   He wore his chest in his coffee   Five Mason
jars

Capped to the brim. Bundled vanilla* ~tubed vanilla~ vanilla extract.

Wore his chest in his coffee, this caffeinated dandy.

I'm thirsty~ Does ice go bad~ I'd better not.

What a luxury it is to weep & mean it.

I bought him this cinnamon from Penzeys Spices in Grand Central
Market.

Bottled wheatgrass; he was spry & juiced for Dakar.

It's bad luck to buy a warm, unsliced pecan pie.

*I'll ask a friend in Salem to ouija vanilla.

COVID permanently closed Penzeys Spices in Grand Central Market.

I might as well dump this box of Arm & Hammer Baking Soda.

Codependent Quarantine

This to say
After blueberries & steel-cut oats:
Please don't fly to LA.
It's just too soon.
The numbers there are rising.
Afraid & afraid for me,
I ask them not to dip
Too deeply into the inkwell
Into the cobalt, into the unsure.
And I grab them & go gentle
& generously into the hour.
I, too, read about American Airlines
Selling-out their flights.

I

Am cautious—

Will

Wear double Black masks
Clean my seat & tray table
With 70% alcohol wipes
& pump hand sanitizer.
My words for miles will be frank.

And

Our snores trace the same night.

But I won't flinch where
This fresh fear has tamed you.

Good & Greasy Gristle

Sunday School Lesson: *Genesis* 19:1-11

of Sodom and Gomorrah

All five of us read two verses.
Like good & greasy gristle

Sister Wooten bit into verse eleven.
Exact lard for the good Lord:

smote…blindness…small and great
Puts a child in the headlock.

"God hosed them with sulfur…"
I'm nine & I lower her volume.

The cemetery grass is green.
Sunday school teacher sees me.

"Prayer heals the scabs in your soul,"
Her right lash bats at my pew.

                    *

I already know
My colors are pink & maroon.

Kayaking at summer camp
Not a note against my will

Chic upended me. The tune,
Good Times.

I aero-flung my hands,
Yells in each hurried snap.

                    *

Until now *Jesus wept*
Blanketed babies & bootleggers.

"Smote." "Blindness."
Soul scabs scare me.

I pray for three straight nights.
I pray for three straight nights.

Syrup-and-ribbon prayers *of* John.
Added trumpets of steeper love.
"God,
I also adore John after practice.

Off the football field.
To him I pen loose-leaf letters.

Tomorrow is Halloween.
Something about this learns to cry."

*

Kayaking at summer camp,
Forward stroke, sweep stroke.
Innocent seating,
Sinless rubs of skin.
Our names pulse
Yes & Yes.

Did my young Jheri curl
Clap that I someday might
Replace angels welcomed by Lot
Fancying night in the city square?
Beatitudes—
Eight blessings rendered
By none other than Jesus
In the Sermon on the Mount
In the Gospel of Matthew.

Next up next Sunday merengue for the meek.

A child launders impossibility.
How were is this?

Cabaret for Freedom **Redux**

—for Dr. Maya Angelou & Godfrey Cambridge

Wrap your head

Slip on the bell bottoms & tank

Strap your sandals

Wear Bakelite bangles

8pm until

If you don't bring it

It won't be there

Director: Ava DuVernay

Executive Producers:
Oprah Winfrey & Tyler Perry

After-Party:
DJ Cassidy

Performers & Speakers

Stacey Abrams	Oleta Adams	Joe Ayoub
Jon Batiste	Angela Bassett	Mary J. Blige
Jericho Brown	Common	Patrisse Cullors
Viola Davis	Fantasia	Tom Ford
Alicia Garza	Farah Jasmine Griffin	Terrance Hayes
André Holland	Bill T. Jones	Samara Joy
John Legend	Don Lemon	Lil Nas X
Lizzo	Dr. Khalil Muhammad	Wangechi Mutu
Suzan-Lori Parks	Gregory Porter	Desmond Richardson
Chris Rock	RuPaul	Sister Sonia Sanchez
Anna Deavere Smith	Mavis Staples	Wanda Sykes
Ayọ Tometi	Kara Walker	Representative Maxine Waters
Lillias White	Kehinde Wiley	Lizz Wright

This Width I'm Wearing Halts
the Cakewalk Song

after Luther Vandross's *You Stopped Loving Me*

Tonight
I caught a glimpse of a sight I'd prejudged:

Child-bearing hips.
I am a man.
The worm crawls out of the apple.

Wrapped in Epsom & Pure-Castile
In no particular formation or logic
Four combs scratch my scalp:

Estrogen, cabana, evening company
Testosterone. I'm whole & complex & funny & here in Tulum.
These combinations never itched.

Or maybe they did

And, so, I double the lather
And increase these wide girls.
Bubbles—they delusion nicely.

Please keep this between us—
I can't tell eating & drinking from atmosphere & ambiance.

I captain cupboards
And turn on the Black music.

No, I just can't get it together.
We row & row & sugar shall win.

What's New at 50?

I roam the planet.
Left the hood late last spring.

I went under the veranda
To ladle the brew.

Alone, nothing aches. This year
In the dream the woman I've seen

Since 12 has one leg & a new porch.
I want a mate who can write my Obituary.

I'm at my retrospective.
Let me call you back.

Thanks & Acknowledgments

Gratitude to editors of the following journals in which variations of these poems first appeared: *The Southern Review, Sazeracs, Smoky Ink, Four Way Review, Transition: Poems in the Afterglow, HIV Here & Now, The Gay & Lesbian Review,* and *Vassar Review.*

Strength and applause to Martha Rhodes and Ryan Murphy for belief in my artistry. Continued thanks to Jonathan Blunk, Hannah Matheson and the all the mighty doers at Four Way Books.

Boundless thanks for your peerless generosity: Purcell Palmer, on two, lengthy occasions, you welcomed me to the Catwalk Art Residency; all I had to do was read & write. I cherish you & our laughter, long talks & Merlot toasts. And beeps to the key cats of Catwalk: Kathy Heins, Shiela Henderson, Victoria Meguin and Chuck Irwin.

Thank you Alan Gilbert, Dorothea Lasky, Nathan McClain and Ricardo Maldonado; it's tricky asking someone to escort your verse into the world.

Pandemic first responders and essential workers, especially my care teams at New York's Lenox Hill Hospital, I thanked you through the nasal cannula & I thank you still.

Aubrey Jackson, Jr., Natalie Weiss and Larry Bentley: I remember.

About the Author

Rodney Terich Leonard is the author of *Sweetgum & Lightning* (Four Way Books), winner of the NCPA Gold Award and the Human Relations Indie Book Award, finalist for the National Indie Excellence Award and semi-finalist for The Poetry Society of Virginia Poetry Book Award. He holds degrees from The New School, NYU Tisch School of the Arts, and Teachers College Columbia University. An Air Force veteran, he received an MFA from Columbia University. He currently lives in Manhattan.

We are also grateful to those individuals who participated in our Build a Book Program. They are:

Anonymous (14), Robert Abrams, Michael Ansara, Kathy Aponick, Michael Anna de Armas, Jean Ball, Sally Ball, Clayre Benzadón, Adrian Blevins, Laurel Blossom, Adam Bohannon, Betsy Bonner, Patricia Bottomley, Lee Briccetti, Joel Brouwer, Susan Buttenwieser, Anthony Cappo, Paul and Brandy Carlson, Dan Clarke, Mark Conway, Elinor Cramer, Kwame Dawes, John Del Peschio, Brian Komei Dempster, Patrick Donnelly, Lynn Emanuel, Blas Falconer, Jennifer Franklin, John Gallaher, Reginald Gibbons, Rebecca Kaiser Gibson, Dorothy Tapper Goldman, Julia Guez, Naomi Guttman and Jonathan Mead, Forrest Hamer, Luke Hankins, Yona Harvey, KT Herr, Karen Hildebrand, Carlie Hoffman, Glenna Horton, Thomas and Autumn Howard, Catherine Hoyser, Elizabeth Jackson, Linda Susan Jackson, Jessica Jacobs and Nickole Brown, Lee Jenkins, Elizabeth Kanell, Nancy Kassell, Maeve Kinkead, Victoria Korth, Brett Lauer and Gretchen Scott, Howard Levy, Owen Lewis and Susan Ennis, Margaree Little, Sara London and Dean Albarelli, Tariq Luthun, Myra Malkin, Louise Mathias, Victoria McCoy, Lupe Mendez, Michael and Nancy Murphy, Kimberly Nunes, Susan Okie and Walter Weiss, Cathy McArthur Palermo, Veronica Patterson, Jill Pearlman, Marcia and Chris Pelletiere, Sam Perkins, Susan Peters and Morgan Driscoll, Maya Pindyck, Megan Pinto, Kevin Prufer, Martha Rhodes and Jean Brunel, Paula Rhodes, Louise Riemer, Peter and Jill Schireson, Rob Schlegel, Yoana Setzer, Soraya Shalforoosh, Mary Slechta, Diane Souvaine, Barbara Spark, Catherine Stearns, Jacob Strautmann, Yerra Sugarman, Arthur Sze and Carol Moldaw, Marjorie and Lew Tesser, Dorothy Thomas, Rosalynde Vas Dias, Rushi Vyas, Martha Webster and Robert Fuentes, Abby Wender and Rohan Weerasinghe, Rachel Weintraub and Allston James, and Monica Youn.